LILIES
of
FORGIVENESS

LILIES *of* FORGIVENESS

A Course in Miracles in Haiku

SANDI CHRISTIE

For my Father

We now begin a spiritual odyssey through the entire text of *A Course in Miracles* one chapter at a time in Haiku. There are over 500 Haiku poems here that highlight some of the greatest spiritual truths ever given to mankind. Enjoy your journey.

ABOUT
A Course in Miracles

A *Course in Miracles* is a self-study spiritual teaching that when understood and practiced can lead to true inner peace, the peace of God. It does not claim to be the only way to God, but it does claim to hasten the journey getting there. The Course uses terminology that is found in Eastern teachings as well as terms that sound distinctly Christian. It should be noted that many of these terms are defined in ways that are nontraditional, so an understanding of *The Text* of *A Course in Miracles* is helpful.

The Preface of *A Course in Miracles* explains how it came about, what it is, and what it says—I invite you to read it if you are not already familiar with the Course. If you do not have a book, you can read it online at the original publisher's (Foundation for Inner Peace) website, www.acim.org.

"Nothing real can be threatened.
Nothing unreal exists.

Herein lies the peace of God." (*ACIM*, T-In.2:2-4)

CHAPTER 1

One is not bigger
Miracles are all the same
Expressions of love

Miracles can heal
Like all expressions of love
They supply a lack

Miracles mean life
God is the giver of life
His Voice will direct

Miracles heal sick
Perception rearranges
Levels not confused

The release from fear
Atoning means undoing
It is essential

A miracle is
Universally blessing
From God to the Son

The revelation
Is the release from all fear
Miracles the means

Miracles praise God
Honoring all creations
Perfection affirmed

Spirit recognized
Miracles adjust levels
Proper alignment

Gratitude not awe
Is all that's necessary
Children are holy

Perceptions askew
Miracles will intercede
Perfection is seen

Illusions dispelled
Freeing the mind from nightmares
The light is perceived

Atoning for lack
They establish perfection
Expressions of love

The Holy Spirit
Recognizes illusions
Without believing

Error is dissolved
The Light of God is perceived
Darkness disappears

It touches many
A miracle is not lost
Undreamed of changes

Time is made shorter
Laws of space time are broken
One is made timeless

Suspension of fear
Revelation induces
Uniting with God

Awe between equals
Is never appropriate
Devotion's needed

Atonement undoes
The error in the mind's eye
Cancelling it out

The meaning is thus
Heaven and earth pass away
No separate states

Those who are released
Forgive brothers in return
They are full of love

Temptation leads not
If errors are recognized
Follow His guidance

Your reality
A graceful state of spirit
Is yours forever

The miracle joins
Placing the mind in service
Of Holy Spirit

Do not wait on time
Time can waste and be wasted
Collapse brings closer

Truth is eternal
It cannot change or be changed
Unalterable

The mind is at choice
It can elect who to serve
It cannot serve two

Stable you are not
Shallow roots need uprooting
They cannot sustain

Original sin
A sense of separation
Must be corrected

If fear is believed
Perfect love will cast it out
It was never real

The mind must be trained
You will need preparation
Or fear will consume

CHAPTER 2

Detour into fear
Occurred through the projection
One mind fragmented

The escape from fear
Requires your mind's acceptance
Of the Atonement

Illness is searching
You cannot find it outside
Health is inner peace

When you are afraid
Remember where your heart is
There your treasure is

If you value wrong
Peace of God denies errors
Darkness into light

We can endure pain
There must be another way
Spiritual Vision

You must look within
Our altar has been defiled
Seek the Atonement

Strength of Its Vision
Brings the mind into service
Restoring power

When you are afraid
Your mind cannot serve Spirit
You must be deceived

A distorted mind
Illness believes in magic
Level confusion

Matter creates not
Only the mind can create
Body the effect

Miracle workers
Must understand fear's release
Accept Atonement

Body does not learn
Only mind illuminates
Look towards the light

Space time readjusts
When you perform miracles
It will be arranged

Fear prevents Spirit
Confuses body with mind
Removes from control

Condone the insane?
Whatever you think- you own
You're responsible

Thought can be guided
It must be given to Him
Stop miscreation

The mind that wanders
Miscreates with a fury
Correct it the same

Strain signifies fear
Your choice must be in accord
Fear will disappear

Conflict is of fear
You have chosen not to love
Perfect love will heal

Thoughts are not idle
All thinking produces form
Thought can move mountains

Miracle working
Entails realization
Thoughts must be guarded

Punishment it's not
The meaning of Last Judgement
Is final healing

God does not punish
Here is the doorway to life
All is One with Him

CHAPTER 3

Atonement teaches
The most perfect of lessons
God is innocence

Nothing can prevail
Against one whose spirit is
Given unto God

The mind awakens
From its sleep and remembers
It's one Creator

You cannot know him
When you attack your brother
You will hurt yourself

Perception's levels
Consciousness was the first split
The ego domain

The mind now confused
Knowledge cannot be perceived
Conflict is induced

When you make something
Separation is believed
Lack is realized

Beyond perception
Knowledge is always stable
It is not doing

Forgiveness heals mind
Separation was perceived
Spirit knows the truth

Judge rather than know
Always leads to loss of peace
It is rejection

Meeting your brothers
Totally without judgement
Tremendous release

Root of all evil
The authority problem
Projects delusions

The problem of peace
The question of authorship
Inheritance lost

Don't depreciate
The real power of your mind
To escape prison

You are choosing death
All those who fear salvation
Death is not the truth

CHAPTER 4

When you are afraid
Be still, know that God is real
You, beloved Son

You've created fear
God was never the author
You have chosen this

Ego is afraid
God is inevitable
Joyous to spirit

Hard to understand
Kingdom of Heaven *is* you
This is Atonement

The Light of God can't
Penetrate the walls you made
To block its entry

Declare your release
God gave you everything
You *are* the Kingdom

If you cannot hear
You're choosing not to listen
Know this need not be

When you feel guilty
Remember the Atonement
Know this need not be

When you feel despair
You are deprived of nothing
Decide otherwise

Seek and ye shall find
The ego has no answer
What is the purpose?

The gift that's needed
Gratitude to your brother
Love sets all things right

Salvation is a
Collaborative venture
Its function is One

God cannot share joy
When his channels are closed off
No rejoice is heard

CHAPTER 5

To heal make happy
The light within you is joy
Gladness is Oneness

Choose wholly joyous
Having and being are same
To have joy give it

The Holy Spirit
Is the spirit of God's joy
Calls you to return

The ego dissolves
From sound of Holy Spirit
But you must choose to hear it

Unwilling to hear
The Voice becomes very weak
The ego delays

Joining Atonement
Is the escape from all fear
Spirit gives meaning

The peace of God is
In your heart and in your hands
To hold and to share

Guilt is not of God
Symbol of attack on Him
And this we believe

Guilt from "the attack"
Fear of retaliation
Projection follows

Mind heals the body
The guiltless mind can't suffer
From sick illusions

Ego speaks judgement
Holy Spirit reverses
The ego is wrong

You can sure delay
Completion of the Kingdom
You cannot bring fear

When joy is absent
You've reacted without love
To one of God's Sons

If you feel guilty
You reinforce the error
It must be undone

You must choose again
Because you are not at peace
Decide otherwise

Choose to be at peace
Holy Spirit will undo
The wrong decision

I choose to let Him
Allowing Him to decide
To choose God for me

CHAPTER 6

Once a thought system
Is developed, it is taught
All teach all the time

The message of the
Crucifixion was that you
Cannot be attacked

You're not a body
Only bodies can be hurt
Spirit does not die

Response of anger
Equates you with a body
Body is not real

Anger is never
Justified if truth is to
Be taught correctly

Belief in bodies
Teaches yourself that you are
Quite destructible

Belief is made real
And is taught to other Sons
They misperceive too

Teach your own perfect
Immunity which is truth
You are not attacked

Teach but only love
For love is all that you are
All else is folly

'Twas a call for peace
Not a weapon for assault
Don't misunderstand

Sins are not punished
Sons of God are not sinners
Do not project blame

Appreciate God
You need this ability
Or you cannot love

You must think like God
If you will know Him again
You cannot be hurt

In separation
Projection reinforces
The split in your mind

Know your perfection
Holy Spirit knows it's true
See it in others

You are part of God
You were never of this world
You are not here now

Return your whole mind
For it has never left Him
This must be perceived

The Kingdom is love
You made the ego without
It does not love you

You are child of God
A priceless part of Kingdom
You have chosen sleep

God calls you to wake
Nothing will be left of dreams
When you awaken

The separation
Communication failure
Has shattered your peace

Children are sleeping
And they must be awakened
If they will know joy

We must wake them up
Children believe in magic
Magic is not real

Sleeping and waking
Realize the difference
Do not fear bad dreams

When the bad dreams come
Call on the light to dispel
You will fear them not

When the ego's gone
Know you will live forever
And death is nothing

Be vigilant for
Only God and His Kingdom
Advanced thought process

You must learn having
Rests on giving not getting
You learn what you teach

CHAPTER 7

The mind misperceives
Sickness and separation
Cannot be of God

Share Holy Spirit
To heal your brother and self
Correct perception

All power is yours
You are the way, truth, and life
Spirit is with you

God has lit your mind
He keeps it lit with His Light
That is what mind is

Spirit works through you
To teach you He is in you
You are part of Him

All abilities
Should be given to Spirit
For proper usage

There is nothing else
But the Kingdom of Heaven
God is all in all

Magic will weaken
The healer becomes special
Understanding lost

The unhealed healer
Seeks gratitude from brothers
But is ungrateful

The mind is changeless
And this must be recognized
In order to heal

Two voices are heard
One way shows you an idol
One way shows the truth

Love is your power
Which the ego must deny
It perceives a threat

One must be chosen
Truth of Light or ego's truth
Or mind will be split

Insanity gives
Opportunity to bless
To receive, you give

This the law of God
No exceptions can there be
To have is to give

Brother is mirror
The reflection of yourself
What you see you are

Unbelievable
Ego will forever be
Dispel the idea

It brings the most joy
But painful to the ego
Listen to Spirit

Happiness is God
Grace is the natural state
Of the Son of God

CHAPTER 8

Hallucination
The belief in the ego
It was never real

Ask and it's given
Because it already has
Been given to you

When you meet someone
It's a Holy encounter
Lose or find yourself

Whenever two meet
Another chance is given
To find salvation

Alone we're nothing
But together our minds fuse
Into great power

Invincible mind
When it is undivided
It's the Mind of God

No separation
Between God and creation
Must be realized

Reach out to my hand
To transcend the ego mind
We need each other

The only question
That should ever be asked is
Do I want God's Will?

Belief in bodies
Produces experience
Of mind's depression

Healing is result
Of using the body for
Communication

Perceive the body
As a separate being
Will foster illness

To communicate
Is to join, but to attack
Is to separate

When others are seen
Limited by the body
So will yourself be

Sickness demonstrates
Your vulnerability
That you can be hurt

A learning device
Is not a teacher, it can't
Tell you how to feel

Do not allow the
Body to be a mirror
Of your own split mind

Only perception
Can be sick because only
Perception errors

When you place limits
On yourself we are not One
And that is sickness

CHAPTER 9

Fear of God's Will is
The strangest belief human
Mind has ever had

You can't distort it
And still have understanding
Of reality

The Christ is in me
And where he is God must be
Christ is part of Him

Because I will to
Know myself I see you as
God's Son, my brother

Your brother's errors
Are not of him and neither
Are your errors real

Accept his errors
And you have attacked yourself
You will pay the price

Only Atonement
Will undo mankind's belief
In separation

You must bring nightmares
To the light of awareness
To teach you they're false

Can you find the light
By analyzing darkness
And making it real?

A therapist does
Nothing, he lets healing be
Trust Holy Spirit

Each part remembered
Adds to your wholeness because
Each part is the whole

Though you're not awake
You can learn to awaken
And help others wake

Grandeur is of God
Therefore, it is inside you
Awareness crucial

Grandiosity
Is only of the ego
Covers for despair

From grandeur you can
Only bless because grandeur
Is your abundance

God is incomplete
No one else can fill your part
In the Mind of God

CHAPTER 10

Law of creation
You must love your creations
As you love yourself

You are home in God
Dreaming of exile and yet
Able to waken

The moment you wake
You will realize fully
The dream was not real

Fearful you must be
Because you have forgotten
Knowledge was replaced

To remember is
To restore the mind to what
Is already there

Belief in sickness
Is to believe that a part
Of God can suffer

Love cannot suffer
Because it cannot attack
Don't side with sickness

Depression is the
Sign of allegiance to him
The god of sickness

Do not forget that
To deny God will result
In your projection

You will believe that
Others have done this to you
Instead of yourself

Allegiance to the
Denial of God is the
Ego's religion

The god of sickness
Demands denial of health
Health opposes it

God will never cease
Loving His Son completely
Would you deny him?

If God knows His Sons
Are wholly sinless, can you
See them as guilty?

CHAPTER 11

You are part of God
God's universe is Himself
Can part be missing?

If you are apart
His Will is not unified
Would God let this be?

Infinity is
Meaningless without His Sons
Do not deny Him

You are but afraid
To know God's Will because you're
Afraid it's not yours

Every symptom
Of sickness and fear begin
In this dark belief

You will never rest
Until you know your function
And make it fulfilled

The Guest God sent you
Will teach you how to do this
If you are willing

Would you be hostage
To the ego, or God's host?
Who will you invite?

When the light comes in
And you say God's Will is mine
You will see beauty

Your way is of pain
That way is hard and lonely
God knows not this way

Blame must be undone
In yourself and in others
Before reaching God

Do not be afraid
To look at the source of fear
Your fear is not real

God is the One Source
What is not of Him does not
Have any power

The ego attacks
It believes it has power
It does nothing else

It's impossible
To see what you don't believe
Those who believe see

You must ask yourself
Do I want this problem solved?
Is answer wanted?

The Holy Spirit
Gives you only what is yours
Asking for nothing

For what is all yours
Is only everything
Shared with all and God

Would you not exchange
Fear for truth if exchange is
Yours for the asking?

CHAPTER 12

To notice error
Is to endow with power
Truth is overlooked

Appreciation
The only appropriate
Response to brother

Only fear and love
Are the emotions of which
You are capable

Miracles translate
Denial into the truth
The light in the fog

Perceive in sickness
But another call to love
Offer only this

Learn to be quiet
In the middle of turmoil
Quietness ends strife

The ego's rule is
Try to learn but don't succeed
Seek but do not find

The ego teaches
How you can gain the whole world
By losing your soul

The Voice for God says
You cannot lose your soul and
The world is nothing

What is One *is* One
The world has no real purpose
Heaven is your home

Guilt is projected
You choose the guide for seeing
Love is extended

When you want just love
You will perceive nothing else
Make love manifest

You have one freedom
The power of decision
You can see it "right"

Accept your mission
By making peace manifest
You must extend it

Undoing your guilt
Is essential to learning
Listen to Spirit

The only way back
To what could never be lost
Is the Atonement

CHAPTER 13

Condemnation is
The root of all attack thoughts
The guilty attack

You can't dispel guilt
By making it real and then
Atoning for it

The real purpose
Of projection is always
To get rid of guilt

All projected guilt
Seems to be concealed and yet
It is still within

Peace is fulfillment
It needs and asks for nothing
Gentleness of love

War asks for it all
And yet nothing can be found
Peace is always lost

47

Do not seek vision
Through the eyes of the body
For this denies light

Miracles allow
The vision of a brother
Without any past

Truth lies in present
Your past was made in anger
Do not seek truth there

Salvation is now
It is the release from time
God's Son is the light

Shine on your brothers
Remember your Creator
Darkness disappears

You do not want it
The world you see disappoints
Do not hold it dear

What you call with love
Will come to you even here
Love always answers

It's impossible
To condemn only a part
Of the brotherhood

Loving only some
Imposes guilt on the whole
Love is not special

It's God's Will that you
Be in Heaven, and nothing
Can keep you from it

CHAPTER 14

The world is insane
Do not underestimate
The insanity

Only truth is true
Nothing else is real at all
Nothing else matters

You must learn this now
Your faith in nothing deceives
Give faith to Spirit

He leadeth me and
Knows the way which I know not
And so I trust Him

When you accept the
Guiltlessness in your brother
You see Atonement

Your function is love
In a dark and loveless place
Darkness is undone

Message is the same
Each teaches differently
God's Son is guiltless

Peace be unto all
Who become teachers of peace
No one's excluded

Exchange dark for light
While ignorance is replaced
With understanding

The search for the truth
Is the removal of things
That will interfere

Light cannot enter
When mind believes in darkness
And won't let it go

Offer guilt to God?
No, you cannot nor can you
Offer it to Son

Reflections of God
Can shine forth healing the world
If mirror is clean

Atonement teaches
How to escape forever
From an unreal past

Do not attempt to
Understand your past events
Darkness will obscure

Darkness will never
Illuminate any of
Your understanding

When peace is threatened
Say I know not what this means
The past is poor guide

Only use the Guide
That God has given to you
Ask and He will guide

CHAPTER 15

Can you imagine
No cares, no worries, just peace
Every moment?

Death is ego's goal
Holy Spirit's goal is life
That which has no end

The belief in hell
Prevents understanding of
The present moment

Ego's use of time
Compounds guilt until it is
All encompassing

Spirit undoes time
It sees no future, no past
Now is forever

Begin to practice
The Holy Instant to teach
Happiness and peace

The Atonement is
In time but is not *for* time
It is eternal

Would you be hostage
To the ego or the host
Of God's magnitude?

You can claim it now
And anytime you want it
The Holy Instant

All separation
Vanishes as holiness
Is shared together

When the Son accepts
The laws of God as his will
He has no limits

The ego believes
That it can get and keep it
By making guilty

The sick attraction
Of guilt must be recognized
For all that it is

Anger is nothing
Except an attempt to make
Someone feel guilty

The ego is the
Symbol of separation
Body its domain

Limit your sight of
A brother to his body
His gifts are denied

You who believe that
Sacrifice is love must learn
Sacrifice brings guilt

If you perceive the
Body as real, you will see
Yourself as deprived

CHAPTER 16

The ego believes
That empathy means joining
In their suffering

The Holy Spirit
Does not join in pain thereby
Sharing delusions

You can't limit hate
Special love relationships
Will not offset it

There is no balance
Between special hate and love
Makes love meaningless

Do not seek for love
Seek to find the barriers
You've built against it

In the name of God
Be willing to abandon
All your illusions

The ego's weapon
Special love relationships
Keep you from Heaven

Every idol
That you raise before you will
Only block the light

Bodies seek to join
And become one by losing
God is left without

The past is long gone
Do not preserve it in dreams
Of retribution

The Holy Instant
Opposes ego's need for
Vengeance for the past

Forgive illusions
You've held against your brothers
They are not valid

Thus you will learn that
By forgiving them you are
Forgiven as well

CHAPTER 17

The betrayal of
The Son of God lies only
In mind's illusions

The real world is found
By complete forgiveness of
The old world you see

God has established
His relationship with you
To make you happy

God's substitute is
The special relationship
The ego's answer

The thought system of
The special relationship
Appears different

Elaborate frame
To divert your attention
From what is enclosed

Look at the *picture*
Do not let the frame distract
Death lies in this gift

"Special" transformed is
The Holy relationship
The old seen anew

You and your brother
Stand together in holy
Presence of the truth

You're joined in purpose
But divided in the means
But the goal is sure

Accept the effects
Of the Holy Instant to
Correct all mistakes

There is no problem
In any situation
That faith will not solve

The Holy Instant
Is the shining example
All seen as a whole

CHAPTER 18

When you see error
Rising to frighten you say
"God's not fear but love"

The truth will save you
Insanity is outside
Sanity's within

Your temper tantrums
Are the dreams in which you scream
"I want it this way!"

Dreams show you that you
Have the power to make a
World as you want it

Yet here is a world
Clearly within your mind that
Seems to be outside

You don't realize
You are making them act out
So they'll be guilty

You seem to waken
But what you awaken to
Is another dream

Your sleeping dreams and
Waking dreams seem different
Content is the same

If you knew who walks
Beside you on your journey
There would be no fear

You and your brother
Are coming home together
After a long trip

A long meaningless
Journey undertook apart
That led to nowhere

The Holy Instant
Requires just your willingness
It is the answer

Everything God
Wills is possible and has
Already happened

The past is long gone
It never really happened
Only in your mind

It is no dream to
Love your brother as yourself
This the happy dream

Heaven's not a place
Nor a condition but just
Awareness of One

One Holy Instant
Together with your brother
Restores universe

When peace comes at last
The realization is
I need do nothing

The body can't "know"
Awareness is limited
God cannot enter

The body is a
Fence around a glorious
And complete Idea

The circle of fear
In which the world is based holds
All your illusions

The insanity
That keeps all the guilt in place
Hidden by the world

CHAPTER 19

Body cannot heal
Its health depends on the mind
It *needs* no healing

The Holy Instant
Shines on the brother and I
The Smile of Heaven

Obstacles to peace
Will come from everywhere
Yet peace will prevail

When the peace in you
Has been extended to all
Spirit's work is done

The first obstacle
The desire to be without
Peace cannot extend

Why keep peace homeless?
This little wall of hatred
Opposes God's Will

Fear not this hindrance
It cannot contain God's Will
Peace will flow across

Your purpose is His
Barriers will fall away
Beneath wings of peace

No illusions stand
Between you and your brothers
Heaven knows you well

Look not on shadows
Shadows cannot hide the sun
The sun has risen

Second obstacle
You value the body for
What it offers you

Here the attraction
Of guilt is made manifest
Seen in the body

You have paid dearly
For your illusions and they
Have not brought you peace

It's impossible
To seek pleasure through body
Without finding pain

Equating yourself
With a body invites guilt
And results in pain

The third obstacle
Is the attraction of death
The ego made death

From the ego came
Sin, guilt, and death to oppose
Life and innocence

Those who fear death miss
How loudly they call to it
To silence God's voice

The fourth obstacle
The fear of God hangs heavy
This the darkest veil

You're afraid of God
Because you fear your brother
You can't love what's feared

CHAPTER 20

Brother is Savior
But if you offer him thorns
You are crucified

Offer him lilies
Look past all your illusions
And set *yourself* free

The way to Heaven
Son has risen from the past
The peace of Easter

Do you like what you
Have made? A world of murder,
Attack and of fear?

You made this world up
It is just your picture of
What you think you are

Nothing can hurt you
Unless you give it power
Illusions have none

Those who choose freedom
Experience only that
Their power is God

The Holy Instant
The gift of God's remembrance
Would you exchange it?

Life's only meaning
Lies in your relationship
To your Creator

All relationships
Of bodies are loveless based
On idolatry

The ego's idol
The belief in sin made flesh
Projected outward

This produces a
Wall of flesh around the mind
Imprisoning it

Keeping it in time
To live but for a moment
To sigh, grieve and die

Salvation is the
Holy Spirit's only goal
The means is Vision

No one who loves can
Judge what he sees, it is free
Of condemnation

Hallucinations
Disappear when they're seen for
What they really are

CHAPTER 21

The world you see is
An outward picture of an
Inward condition

How foolish it is
To attempt to judge but what
Vision could show you

I'm responsible
For the world I see and all
That seems to happen

No accidents nor
Chance is possible within
God's reality

When Vision's denied
Confusion of cause and effect
Become possible

Faith, belief, Vision
These the means that are needed
Holiness is reached

Perception selects
And makes the world that you see
As the mind directs

Reason can't see sin
but it can see errors, and
Leads to correction

You are his savior
Your brother is also yours
Heaven is assured

All your misery
Comes from the strange belief that
You are powerless

Being helpless is
The cost of sin, helplessness
Is sin's condition

Do I desire a
World I rule instead of one
That seems to rule me?

Do I desire a
World where I am powerful
Instead of helpless?

Do I want a world
Where I have no enemies
And there is no sin?

And do I want to
See what I denied *because*
It is the whole truth?

Happiness changing
Form that shifts with time and place
Is an illusion

Constant joy is a
Condition alien to
Your understanding

CHAPTER 22

Who has need for sin?
Only the lonely who see
But differences

A holy union
Sees no lack within, nothing
That needs be taken

Illusions carry
Guilt, suffering, and sickness
Death to believers

Reason will tell you
To escape from misery
Go the other way

One illusion held
Defended against the truth
Makes truth meaningless

There is no part of
Heaven you can take and weave
Into illusions

Nor are there any
Illusions you can take and
Enter Heaven with

Reason and ego
Are contradictory and
Cannot coexist

The ego's whole plan
Depends on its belief that
You can't learn this Course

A holy Union
However newly born must
Value holiness

How are illusions
Overcome? Not by force, not
By opposition

By letting reason
Tell you that they contradict
True reality

Do you want freedom
Of the body or of mind?
You cannot have both

Freedom of body
Has no meaning so the mind
Must serve illusions

The Holy Spirit
But waits in gentle patience
Certain of outcome

The holy Union
Lovely in its innocence
Mighty in its strength

If Oneness with God
Were recognized you would know
His power is yours

The light that joins you
With your brother shines throughout
The whole universe

And so this light that
Joins you both makes you both One
With your Creator

CHAPTER 23

He walks in peace who
Travels sinlessly along
The way love shows him

They share love's strength for
They looked on innocence and
Errors disappeared

God's memory comes
Gently to the quiet mind
Where conflict is not

Do you know that a
War against yourself would be
A war against God?

Illusions battle
With themselves and yet truth is
Indivisible

There is nothing you
Can attack that is not but
A part of yourself

The laws of chaos
Can be brought to the light but
Never understood

First law of chaos
That the truth is different
For everyone

Principle maintains
A belief in hierarchy
Of all illusions

Next law of chaos
All must sin, suffer, die, and
Be punished for sin

This leads to third law
Of chaos that seems to make
Chaos eternal

There is no release
And no escape, and vengeance
Is the Will of God

Fourth law of chaos
This is the belief you have
What you have taken

Another's loss is
Your gain without knowing that
It's taken from you

Last law of chaos
Holds there is a substitute
For love that will cure

These laws hold in place
The substitute for Heaven
That you must prefer

Can condemnation
Bless you or can attack in
Any form be love?

Do not mistake truce
For peace, nor compromise for
Escape from conflict

The overlooking
Of the battleground is now
Your only purpose

CHAPTER 24

Love is extension
It offers everything
Now and forever

Only the special
Could have enemies for they
Appear different

What is different
Calls for judgement and must come
From someone "better"

Specialness then sets
Apart and serves as grounds for
Justified attack

Those who are special
Must defend their illusions
But against the truth

Comparison must
Be an ego device for
Love could not make this

Defend specialness
You can, but you will not hear
The Voice for God there

Forgiveness is but
The ending of specialness
Illusions released

The special ones sleep
Lost in dreams of specialness
They don't hear God's call

Specialness is a
Lack of trust in anyone
Except for yourself

Everything else
Becomes your enemy to
Be feared and attacked

In the world of dreams
Effect and cause are reversed
Dreamer is the dream

The Christ in you is
Very still, his love for God
Replaces your fear

Look on your brother
Don't let specialness obscure
The truth within him

Perception can serve
Another goal, you can make
A different choice

CHAPTER 25

The body needs none
But the mind requires healing
From body belief

You're the means for God
Not separate, nor with a
Life apart from His

Father and Son and
Holy Spirit are as One
Joined as One in truth

What's the same can't be
Different, what is One can't
Have separate parts

Accept God's own frame
In place of yours and you'll see
God's own masterpiece

Within the darkness
See the savior *from* the dark
Behold holiness

All here have entered
Darkness, and yet no one has
Entered it alone

Can misperception
Be a sin? Let all brother's
Errors be nothing

The sun in you has
Now risen and in the light
You will stand in peace

Wholly unafraid
From you this peace will extend
Darkness into light

The grace of God rests
Gently on forgiving eyes
No evil is seen

The Holy Spirit
Needs your special function so
His may be fulfilled

To be just is to
Be fair and not be vengeful
Offer miracles

CHAPTER 26

The world seen is a
Picture of disunity
And lack of joining

Ask for sacrifice
God's memory is denied
No song of Union

Every instant
You can be reborn and be
Given life again

If God is just, then
There can be no problems that
Justice cannot solve

How great your release
Will be when you're willing to
Receive correction

Complexity is
Not of God, how could it be
All He knows is One

There's a borderland
Where illusions are laid down
Here the journey ends

Heaven was not lost
And so it cannot be saved
Undo illusions

Forgiveness turns a
World of sin into a world
Wonderful to see

Each flower shines in
Light and every bird sings
The joy of Heaven

In this holy place
You stand where sin has left and
The face of Christ seen

You have two choices
Go toward Heaven, or go
Away to nowhere

God gave His teacher
To replace the one you made
Not to conflict with

The time of terror
Was undone so long ago
It stands corrected

Time is but the mad
Belief that what is over
Is still here and now

All sickness comes from
Belief in separation
Denied, it will go

In the world of sin
Guilt asks for punishment and
Request is granted

Ideas are of mind
They leave not their source although
They seem external

Nothing gives meaning
Where no meaning is and who
Looks there is deceived

Sins are just beliefs
That you impose between your
Brother and yourself

CHAPTER 27

Walk the gentle way
And you will fear no evil
No shadows at night

The pain you suffer
Is proof that your brother is
guilty of attack

You are a symbol
A testament of his guilt
Closing Heaven's gate

The unhealed cannot
Pardon for they witness that
Pardon is unfair

No one can forgive
A sin he believes is real
He holds proof of sin

Miracles bestow
The release from guilt from both
Your brother and you

Only in stillness
Is everything answered
All problems resolved

A broken body
Shows the mind has not been healed
Proves separation

Healing miracle
Proves that the separation
Is without effect

The Holy Instant
Is where the miracle lives
An instant of love

Pain does demonstrate
That the body must be real
Obscures Spirit's Voice

Pleasure and pain are
Equally unreal for their
Witness is the same

You are the dreamer
Of the world of dreams, hear the
Call to awaken

No one reacts to
Figures in a dream unless
They believe they're real

You believe others
Have done to you what you think
You have done to them

"Innocence" is kept
By pushing guilt out of you
Seeing it in them

Salvation's secret
Is only that you're doing
This unto yourself

You would not react
To figures in a dream if
You knew you're dreaming

You need only learn
Both of you are innocent
Or both are guilty

CHAPTER 28

Miracles cancel
They merely take away
The effects of guilt

The Holy Spirit
Can make use of memories
For God is still there

The Holy Spirit
Uses memory as a
Way to let it go

What *you* remember
Never was, it can only
Deserve your laughter

The miracle comes
Quietly into the mind
That stops and is still

Memory of God
Arises in the mind that
Has no fear of Him

The cause of healing
Is cause of everything
It has *one* Effect

The miracle does
Not waken you, it shows you
Who the dreamer is

The miracle shows
You dream a dream and that its
Content is not true

Miracles stand in
Shining silence next to all
Dreams of guilt and pain

The miracle does
Nothing because minds are joined
And can't separate

The end of dreaming
Is the end of all your fear
Love was never there

Separation is
The cause of pain, the body
Is just the effect

God can never bridge
All the seeds of your sickness
Or the shame of guilt

Do not be afraid
Light your world with miracles
Join your brother there

Accept Atonement
Means do not support dreams of
Sickness and of death

Your brother believes
He is a dream, do not share
In his illusions

It is their sharing
Dreams of suffering and pain
That makes them seem real

No one can suffer
If he does not see himself
Attacked and losing

Sickness is anger
Taken out on the body
So it suffers pain

God asks for nothing
His son need ask for nothing
For there is no lack

Yet faithlessness is
The house set upon the straw
It is not stable

CHAPTER 29

There's no time, no place,
No state where God is absent
Nothing to be feared

It's the fear of God!
The greatest obstacle that
Peace must flow across

Hopeless to attempt
To find any hope of peace
On a battleground

Make the way for love
You did not create it but
You can extend it

You can't dream some dreams
And wake from some, for you are
Sleeping or awake

There's a place in you
Where the world is forgiven
Illusions are gone

Seek not outside self
It will fail and you will weep
When an idol falls

Idols of the world
Were made to keep truth hidden
Keeping dreams in place

Their form deceives you
Idols are substitutes for
Your reality

You believe idols
Will complete your little self
You give them power

What is an idol?
Nothing! The miracle lifts
The veil and truth shines

A dream of judgement
Entered into God's Son's mind
Heaven changed to hell

How does God's Son wake
From the dream? He must judge not
And he will waken

You but dream a dream
Idols the toys you play with
You pretend they're real

You have forgotten
You made up the dream in which
Your toys appear real

Forgiving dreams will
Show you that you're safe and have
Not attacked yourself

CHAPTER 30

The new beginning
The goal is clear, specific
Methods are needed

Constant decisions
You are always making them
Do not be the judge

Think about what kind
Of day you would like to have
Know you can have it

The outlook starts with
Today I won't make any
Decisions myself

Your problem is this
You make up your mind and *then*
Ask what you should do

Do you understand
Opposing Holy Spirit
Is to fight *yourself?*

And Heaven itself
Represents your will, all was
Created for you

Beyond all idols
Is the thought God holds of you
Always as it was

You will attack what
Does not suit you not seeing
That you made it up

Never in time did
Idols bring you anything
But the gift of guilt

Idolatry's proof
Your belief in a sickness
Forgiveness won't heal

I thank you Father
For your perfect Son, I see
My glory in him

A constant purpose
The one thing that gives events
A stable meaning

A common purpose
Is the means where perception
Can be stabilized

Reality is
Changeless, it cannot deceive
It transcends all form

What is temptation?
Only the wish to make your
Illusions seem real

See the Christ in him
Let there be no dreams that you
Would prefer to see

CHAPTER 31

Simple salvation!
What was never true is not
And never will be

Salvation declares
What is false cannot be true
Truth cannot be false

You hate your brother
Not for his sins against you
But for your own sins

Learn without despair
There's no answer in the world
Do not seek hope there

Your own self concept
It bears no likeness to you
It is an idol

You either see flesh
Or you recognize Spirit
There's no compromise

If flesh is chosen
You won't escape the body
As reality

If you choose Spirit
Heaven bends to touch your eyes
Blessing holy sight

What is temptation?
Only the wish to stay in
Hell and misery

Temptation teaches
The Holy Son of God is
A body that dies

He cannot escape
Its frailty, its limits or
Its tiny power

So choose once again
Take your place among saviors
Or remain in hell

Trials are lessons
That you failed to learn before
Presented again

In all your distress
Christ but calls to you gently
Brother choose again

He will not leave you
Comfortless in dreams of hell
He'll release your mind

God's Son can't suffer
He is as God created
And you *are* His Son

A miracle comes
To heal God's Son, closing door
On dreams of weakness

No darkness remains
To obscure the face of Christ
The Light lives in you

We have reached Our home
In Your likeness Our Light shines
Thy Will is now done

Now we say Amen
No more faith in illusions
When we are all One

ABOUT THE AUTHOR

Sandi Christie is the author of *Miracles Fall Like Drops of Rain—Inspired poetry from A Course in Miracles Workbook for Students.* She has been a student of *A Course in Miracles* since the mid 1990's, and is an advocate of the teachings of Kenneth Wapnick, Ph.D.